I am Grace Stone

Tracy Briscoe

Presentation by *BookLeaf Publishing*

Web: www.bookleafpub.com

E-mail: info@bookleafpub.com

ISBN: 9789357617109

First edition 2022

To the Sun and the Moon.

Deeply Today

Feel deep
Feel deep today
Dive, reach, delve
In who you are today.

Move deep
Move deep into the dark
Crawl, scramble, claw
In who you are today.

See deep
See deep into the heart
Break, open, breathe
In who you are today.

Hear deep
Hear deep into the soul
Grasp, listen, grow
In who you are today.

Feel love
Feel love today
Pray, hope, praise
In who you are today.

See light
See light in the dark
Fly, soar, fill
In who you are today.

Believe
There is light in the dark
Believe, in who you are
Deeply today

Remember, Alone

I remember,
Me in a field lying in the grass, running down a
grassy hill.
Rowing a boat on the pond.
Skating on dad's homemade ice rink, with a
single street lamp, singing my heart out.
Looking up through the apple orchard trees.
Snowshoeing when the sun is going down, in my
own backyard.
And,
I remember,
My best moments are when I am alone, away
from others.
I found solace in the outdoors, singing loudly,
alone.
I will find these moments, everyday!
But,
I remember,
Alone does not mean ALONE, not connected
Alone means, it is okay to step away from others
energies.
When I ask for time out or to be given some
space, it does not mean that I am angry, that I am
sad, that I do not love you.

It is because I love you, that I ask for that
ALONE time.
A chance, an opportunity for me to connect with
myself.
A chance, an opportunity to be grateful, to
remember all the things that bring joy.
Those connections.
So that I can keep creating my best, joyful,
moments.
Time to be, to receive, to reflect, to shed, to feel,
to love, to give thanks.
To remember.
Find your best, most joyful moments!
Those moments when you feel whole.
Connect.
Remember to live them.

Open Your Eyes

Open your eyes
See what resides
Dig deep inside
Let your heart free your mind
Find your own place
Get out of the race
Go at your own pace
Create your own space
Where your free to care
No judgement there
No shame to share
Oh, let down your hair
Bet you didn't know
How the power does flow
Now let it show
How much you glow
Open your eyes
See what resides
Dig deep inside
Let your heart free your mind
Find your own place
Create your own space
Where your free to care
Oh, let down your hair
Bet you didn't know

How much you glow
Open your eyes
Let your heart free your mind
Open your eyes
Let your heart free your mind
Let your heart free your mind

Drum Call

Oh, oh ,ohm
My sisters, come
When I beat my drum
A Goddess embrace
Angels hold my space
Taking me to Mother Earth
The home of my birth
While healers wash my fears away
And
This is what they say
'Hold our hands
Dance around the fire
Raise your arms
You will soar higher'
Wake up, wake up sleepy head
Wake up, wake up is what they said
Oh, oh, ohm
My sisters, come
When I beat my drum.

Heartbeat

The Earth I hold in my hands,
The Air blows around me, as I breathe,
The Water reminds me to just flow,
A Fire burns, inside of me.

Part of my heart
My heartbeat

The Earth will nourish with her life,
The Air will whisper what it knows,
The Water reflects back an image true,
The Fire protects and will never burn.

Part of my heart
My heartbeat.

My heartbeat.

The Truth

Like a bird
But not frail
A voice that sings out,
Loud and clear
A bird
Oh so sweet
Yet would rather hide than be heard, or seen
Heart that is full and vulnerable
And, has been hurt many, many times
Remember you are loved, so much
Remember that love and give love to yourself
Remember to eat, nourish
Be like a bird, protect your heart, your nest
The nest you reside in with a Soul's dream
Be like a bird, learn to fly free
Learn to use your wings
Be ready to soar
Ready to be
Ready to heal
Ready to sing
Ready for the Truth
The Truth about you.

Rose Scented Paper

Garden of delights
Hold me in your sights
Beauty everywhere
Embrace me in your care
As a scent washes over me
Like a whisper on the breeze
So here I read my prayer
Written on rose scented paper

Rose scented paper
Rose scented paper

Reveling in this space
Basking in your grace
Magic everywhere
Spirit gifts to share
As the flowers open wide
The colours warm me up inside
So here I read my prayer
Written on rose scented paper

Rose scented paper
Rose scented paper

Through the air
Hear my prayer.

Stay, Witch

The shoes you wear
They are your own
The don't know
The past you were born, in
Strange
Little girl
Let them judge
It's not about you
To your heart
You must be true, and
Weird
Little girl
And reach in
And begin
And grow stronger
Sweet daughter
Stay, Witch
Step into the circle, and
You will learn
To let your light
Flow
Little girl
Take a breath
Reach deep
Feel the Earth

Beneath you feet, and
Smile
Little girl
Stay, Witch
And reach in
And begin
And grow stronger
Sweet daughter
Stay, Witch
Stay, Witch.

Ode to the Moon

Even in the darkest of darks
As the black clouds roll through
There is light
Time to hunt, to pluck up each hurt and pain
Examine them carefully
Acknowledge each one
Bow to them
Recognize their worth
Without them, you would not be here
Now
At this moment
With this breath
With that drum
Beating inside of you
Each pain has been a gift
Each hurt has shown your strength and worth
Your light
So remember
When you are in the dark
Take your time
Welcome the feeling, the experience
Face it with grace
Beat your drum
Say 'Thank you'
Light will come
An ode to the moon.

Moments

Sit on the grass and take in the views
The mist rising over the fields, of yellow and
brown hues
Everything is evolving, changing, moment by
moment you see
The Universe is trying to give life back, to
humanity
Teachings of, worry less about the future and
what it may bring
Live more in the moment and listen, your heart
will sing
Teachings of, let go of the past, it is not who you
are
Live more in the moment and feel, your soul
will remember you are a star
Inhale deep take in all that is around you and
exhale slow
The Universe teachings are what you need to
know
Less worry of the future, no more fear of the
past
This is your life, live it, like it may be your last
Moment, by moment, by moment, by moment...

I Am Home

I am, I am, I am
A life, a love, a light
Shining bright
A life, a love, a light
Shining bright
I am
Awake and now I see
How I want to be
Feeling the energy
As it flows through me
I am, I am, I am
A life, a love, a light
Shining bright
A life, a love, a light
Shining bright
I am
Guided to happiness
Rooted in wholeness
Powerful presence
Of Divine essence
I am, I am, I am
A life, a love, a light
Shining bright
A life, a love, a light
Shining bright

I am
Connected and have grown
My soul is being shown
The way and I have flown
My spirit is coming home
I am, I am, I am
A life, a love, a light
Shining bright
A life, a love, a light
Shining bright
I am
I am
I am home.

Write your Story

Wouldn't you love to write your story?
Of your hopes, dreams and glory
A flow to help you find
The connection of heart to mind
And as you sit with that thought, today
Carry it, as you go your way
A life force of energy
Releasing what you no longer need
So
Wouldn't you love to write your story?

Autumn Wind Dance

Sit quietly
Drink a tea
Feel the warmth of the autumn sun
Enjoy the heat
See beyond your own space
Watch the trees swaying
The long, tall grass bending
Watch them give way
Listen to the trees and the rustling leaves
Hear the chimes in the distance
Know that it is the wind
The trees, the grass, the leaves and the chimes
Are all bending, softening, moving
To allow the wind through
To allow and make way
For release
The release of a branch, a grass seed or a falling
leaf
The wind is doing it's dance
And like a tree, the grass or the leaves
You need to bend, to soften to move
To allow and make way
For release
The release of a whisper, a sigh or a cry
Allow the wind to blow and lift you

To take you on it's dance
Drop that branch, release that seed, let the leaves
fall, whisper, sigh or cry
The wind will carry it away, for release
Let it go.
The autumn wind dance.

A Morning Prayer

I sing to the spirit of the sky
I sing to the spirit of the land
I am calling you
East, South
West and North
You surround me
The cool of the air and,
The warmth of the fire
Taking my vibe higher
I feel the Earth beneath my feet
The water cleanses me clean
Taking me through life's flow
East, South
West and North
You surround me
I sing to the spirit of the sky
I sing to the spirit of the land
I am calling you
A thank you, a thank you
A thank you

Hold the Light

As I wonder, I sit and ponder
What is life, with so much strife?
In me
Life is a beautiful place, filled with love, joy and
grace
Rolled into one, just like the sun
In me

Look into your heart
You will find the light
Take it with you
To each and every fight

In the past, I moved too fast
I wasn't strong, some choices wrong
In me
But each of them, a lesson, a gem
I hold them tight, they bring the might
In me

Look into your heart
You will find the light
Take it with you
To each and every fight

I would say, led astray
Those words were fake, the heart did break
In me
As I hit each wall, I climbed them all
I'll never fear it, can't break the spirit
In me

Look into your heart
You will see the light
Take it with you
To each and every fight

In me

Grace

It doesn't matter
What brought you here
All that matters is
That you are here

The need to share or explain
That is ego
Not needed here
What you bear is heavy for you

I only want to hold your hand
Sit with you in silence
No one is here to compare, nor judge
No one is here to tell you it will be alright, either

I am here, only, to love you
Here to hold you up
To be with you in crisis, sorrow, worry, fear and
joy
This is grace

If you have read this far

You are supported
You are loved
You are on your way to grace
Believe that.

Creation

Acknowledge, embrace
You are from creation
Place this seed, within
Within your heart
You will be led
To scribe
To write
To recite
To dance
To sing
Creatively
We are all born to create
Place that seed, within
Within your heart
Will you sing?
Will you dance?
Will you write?
Will you paint?
Will you draw?
What will you create?
We are all artists
Creatively
And
Collectively, we share ourselves
Through
Creation

Child of Mine

Afraid of the rise because of the fall
You could see the path, but, chose to crawl
Burdened by guilt and another's shame
Wrestling with a fear, which you could never
name
Child of mine.

They are not you and you are not them, to be
And that, my love,is all you need to see
You arrive, you honour, you cherish and
sometimes you leave
And always follow what you believe
Child of mine.

You take and you give
Remembering, you are here to live
To be in the moment, the here and the now
Be brave, be strong, be soft, be loving and never
back down
Child of mine.

Be honest, be forgiving and be true
Especially to yourself, to you
This is your time, you are free and will shine
My divine
Child of mine.

Healing

Healing
To move forward, to step away from the past
To no longer carry what has been left behind
Generationally

Healing
To no longer worry of changes that this World
may see
To understand that everything is evolving,
rotating, a cycle, a circle
Patterning

Healing
To stop judging others and the paths they choose
To realize we need all skills of religion, science,
reason, politics, military
Accepting

Healing
To find life direction, a soul's purpose
To achieve what is 'most' good
Living

Healing

To be present in shared spaces and be with loved
ones
To understand joy, peace and grace, with loved
ones, unconditionally
Loving

Healing
To beat at the highest frequency, of love
To share this love with the World
Vibing

Healing

The Three Sisters

Looking in the mirror, deep into the eyes that
have known
A Maiden, a Mother and how she has grown
The Maiden, who grew up in a trauma filled
home
To become the Mother, dealing with children
and problems of her own
Now, while looking in the mirror, she traces
every wrinkle and notices all the grey growing
in
Finally, loving herself, in her own skin
Acknowledging the Maiden who was scarred by
judgement, in her life
Honouring the Mother who couldn't see past the
scars, blaming them for her hardships and strife
Now, while looking in the mirror, she sees her
truest self and feels so strong
Finally, living a life that has taken so long
As she watched the Maiden who had no desire to
live, no dreams, no will to try
And the Mother, to live, she would just mutter
under her breathe, sigh and cry
Now, while looking in the mirror, she lives each
moment with zest

Finally, committing to life, the life held tight in
her breast

She is the Crone

Coming into her own
She will sing you a beautiful song
Gathering nature as she hums along
She is a wonderful sight to see
Holding the maiden and the mother tenderly
As each have played such and important part
In creating the enormity of her heart
She basks in this knowledge, in her aged
wisdom, as the mirror reflects the sun
It shines in her eyes and she knows she is a
loved one
Cradling the Maiden and the Mother, the
sweetest sisters she has ever known
As the protective, loving, ever evolving,
beautiful Crone.